DARING WOMEN

25 WOMEN WHO RULED

Rebecca Stanborough

COMPASS POINT BOOKS
a capstone imprint

Compass Point Books are published by Capstone Press
1710 Roe Crest Drive, North Mankato, Minnesota 56003
www.mycapstone.com

Library of Congress Cataloging-in-Publication Data
Library of Congress Cataloging-in-Publication data is available on the Library of Congress website.

ISBN 978-0-7565-5851-2 (hardback)
ISBN 978-0-7565-5868-0 (paperback)
ISBN 978-0-7565-5856-7 (eBook PDF)

Editorial Credits
Anna Butzer, editor; Russell Griesmer, designer; Jennifer Bergstrom, production artist;
Svetlana Zhurkin, media researcher; Laura Manthe, production specialist

Photo Credits
AP Photo: David Guttenfelder, cover; Capstone Press: 18, 27, 37; Dreamstime: Laurence Agron, 51; Getty Images: AFP/ Aamir Qureshi, 14, Bettmann, 55, Robert R. McElroy, 39, The LIFE Images Collection/Bob Peterson, 23; Library of Congress, 29; Newscom: akg-images, 11, Icon Sportswire/John Korduner, 49, MCT/Abaca Press/Olivier Douliery, 21, Polaris/ Baldev Kapoor, 17, Polaris/i-Images/Dinendra Haria, 25, Reuters/Ivan Alvarado, 19, Reuters/Lucas Jackson, 35, Reuters/ Philippe Wojazer, 33, Reuters/Stephen Lam, 36, Sipa/Romuald Meigneux, 31, Zuma Press/Christy Bowe, 53; Shutterstock: 360b, 9, Andrea Delbo, 44, Banana Oil, 4–5, DFree, 46, Jaguar PS, 41, Leonard Zhukovsky, 57, Shaun Jeffers, 7, Twocoms, 43; Wikimedia: Margaret Thatcher Foundation/Chris Collins, 12

Design Elements by Shutterstock

For Paris, who ruled at Murray Middle School

Printed in the United States of America.
PA017

— TABLE OF CONTENTS —

INTRODUCTION

Women rulers are heroic. They have led nations, fought for freedom, created great works of art, built companies, smashed records, opened doors of opportunity, and inspired millions of people. Some were born into powerful families and inherited great wealth. Some knew what it was like to be hungry or homeless. Every one of them worked hard to achieve her dreams. Every one of them changed the world.

Women rulers throughout history have changed the world.

Chapter 1

WOMEN WHO RULED FOR DECADES

Few people can imagine what it is like to be responsible for the welfare of an entire country. These women didn't have to imagine it. They ruled nations. They appointed cabinets, negotiated with foreign diplomats, started and ended wars, and made daily decisions that changed the lives of millions. These women rocked the world.

Elizabeth II
(1926–)
Queen of England

Princess Elizabeth was awake in the early morning hours. She stood at the window of the treehouse, watching the elephants at the watering hole below.

"They're pink," she said.

The elephants had been rolling in Kenya's colorful dust. At that moment, watching elephants in the moonlight, the young woman had no idea she had become queen of England.

She would assume the tremendous responsibility the next day, when she learned that her beloved father, King George VI, had died. In the 65 years since then, Queen Elizabeth II has steadied the nation in an era of great change. During her reign, more

Queen Elizabeth II, 2012

than 40 colonies gained independence to form new nations. She has worked with 13 different prime ministers and countless other politicians with widely varying political views. She has taken 271 trips to 128 nations across the globe.

What has remained constant throughout her reign is her commitment to duty and service. She begins nearly every day with a review of her renowned red boxes, which contain reports on the actions of Parliament, important letters, and governmental documents.

"I must go do my boxes," she has told friends. "If I missed one once, I would never get it straight again."

Her schedule remains challenging. She meets with people from all over the world almost every day. She lends her support to charities and attends countless events of all sorts. And while some of these duties may seem merely ceremonial, her participation in the life of the nation unifies an increasing population. As Britain's longest-reigning monarch, she has received her share of criticism. But she is almost universally admired for her dedication to serving people with intelligence and wit.

Angela Merkel
(1954–)
Chancellor of Germany

Angela Merkel grew up in a divided nation surrounded by walls. West Germany was a free, democratic society. But in East Germany, where Angela Merkel and her family lived, a strict communist government controlled jobs, housing, and education. Those who disagreed with the government found themselves out of a job, cut off from schooling, or imprisoned.

Angela Merkel's father was a Lutheran pastor in an atheist nation, and her family was under constant surveillance. A 103-mile (165-kilometer) concrete wall through Berlin separated east from west Germany. In the wall's 28-year history, nearly 200 people were killed trying to escape. Germany was reunited as a democratic nation in 1990. But growing up in a family whose values clashed with the government may have given Merkel a lasting gift. She developed an ability to cautiously consider all solutions to a problem before deciding what to do. Or maybe being analytical was simply her nature: She was trained as a mathematician and physicist.

Angela Merkel was elected the first female chancellor of Germany in 2005.

Angela Merkel at a press conference after a meeting with the NATO Secretary General in the Federal Chancellery in Berlin, June 2016

She is still chancellor today. She has guided Germany through two serious crises. The first was the economic crash that struck Europe in 2008. Merkel's carefully considered policies made Germany the strongest economy in Europe at a time when other nations buckled.

In 2015 and 2016, disasters in Syria and Libya caused millions to flee their homelands in the largest human migration in modern history. Under Merkel's leadership, Germany opened its doors to the refugees. Speaking of these refugees, Merkel said, "[I]t is not masses that arrive but individuals. For every human being has the dignity which is given to him by God."

Indira Gandhi
(1917–1984)
Prime Minister of India

Indira Gandhi grew up in a family of daring activists. During India's quest for independence from British rule, her family members were jailed many times. She was so accustomed to hearing about protests that she made them part of her childhood games. She would set up two groups of dolls, freedom fighters and police, and enact confrontations between them. Later, her imaginative play became reality. She was jailed for speaking out against the British Raj, the British rulers of India, when she was 24 years old.

India gained independence in 1947. Gandhi's father, Jawaharlal Nehru, was elected prime minister. She shadowed him as he met with world leaders and made decisions about India's future. It was excellent training. In 1966 Gandhi was elected the first female prime minister of India, the largest democracy in the world.

In the years that followed, the people of India alternately adored and hated Gandhi. They loved her for skillfully executing a 14-day war to free neighboring Bangladesh from Pakistani rule. She was compared to Durga, a powerful and protective Hindu goddess. But later she was hated with equal strength.

Gandhi's government was accused of

corruption. Some officials took huge bribes for favors. Drought brought hunger, and people felt she didn't do enough to help. When a court ruled that Gandhi had rigged an election, she declared a state of emergency instead of leaving office. She had her opponents arrested. She suspended rights such as freedom of speech and freedom of the press. When she finally allowed another election, she lost.

Countless Berliners greeted Indira Gandhi during her visit to East Berlin in 1976.

Years later she was elected prime minister again. The people of India forgave Gandhi's earlier failures. But there was one group of citizens she deeply offended. India's Punjab state was home to many people in the Sikh religion. Some Sikhs wanted to separate and form their own nation. Gandhi wanted India to remain united. She had the army raid their temple. The soldiers killed hundreds of people and nearly destroyed the holy place.

In revenge, two of Gandhi's Sikh bodyguards assassinated her in 1984. She was mourned by millions, and is remembered for the heights and depths she reached as a leader.

Margaret Thatcher, 1989

Lady Margaret Thatcher
(1925–2013)
Prime Minister of England

The 24-year-old candidate stepped onto the soapbox, looking somewhat out of place among the bricklayers of Dartford. The crowd paid attention—whether because of her fierce speech or from the novelty of seeing a female candidate. Margaret Roberts was in her element. She had been listening to political debates since her childhood. Though she was trained at Oxford University as a chemist, it was politics that thrilled her.

When Margaret Thatcher took office as prime minister in 1979, Britain was still reeling from a period of economic trouble they called the "Winter of Discontent." Inflation was at a staggering 10 percent, making it hard for ordinary citizens to afford the necessities of life. Over 1 million people were out of work, and some trade unions had gone on strike. Even gravediggers and trash collectors were refusing to work until their demands were met.

Thatcher was a lifelong conservative. She and the Conservative Party believed that it was a mistake for people to depend on the government for financial help. Conservatives also believed that government needed to be small to make room for private companies to grow and to employ people. At first, conservative policies led to a deeper recession in England, and Thatcher's approval ratings sank.

But the economy eventually rebounded, and Thatcher's sharp reduction in government spending and tight rein on unions became more appreciated. When she went to war to protect the Falkland Islands—a British territory—her popularity rose even more. A Soviet diplomat once called her the "Iron Lady," and the nickname stuck.

Though she eventually resigned her position in the face of opposition during her third term, she was the longest-serving British prime minister in the 20th century. She served in the House of Lords until her death at age 87.

> *Don't follow the crowd, let the crowd follow you.*
> –Margaret Thatcher

Benazir Bhutto waved to her supporters during a rally in the port city of Karachi, Pakistan, February 1999.

Benazir Bhutto
(1953–2007)
Prime Minister of Pakistan

Prime Minister Benazir Bhutto stood atop a glacier in Siachen, the highest point in Pakistan, listening to a military briefing. She was surrounded by snowy peaks—and the Indian army was encamped just across the Gyong La Pass. In this, the world's highest battleground, the prime minister was keeping a secret. She was going to have a baby.

Weeks later, when news got out, Bhutto found herself on a different kind of battlefield. Some people argued that she couldn't lead the country while she was pregnant. She gave birth to her child and returned to work the next day.

Bhutto was the first democratically elected female prime minister of a Muslim nation. Her father, Prime Minister Zulfikar Ali Bhutto, had helped modernize Pakistan, opening opportunities for women and minorities. However, his progressive ideas did not sit well with everyone. When Bhutto was a young woman, her father was assassinated.

For the next decade, Bhutto and thousands of other Pakistanis were jailed for opposing the government. Many were tortured and killed. Despite years of imprisonment, she did not give in to those who demanded that she withdraw from public service.

In 1988 when elections were finally permitted again, Bhutto won by a landslide. Right away, she began working toward democracy. She lifted the ban on labor unions. She restored freedom of the press and freed political prisoners. Her government brought electricity, clean water, and phone service to remote villages. She even reached out to build peace with India. She was elected to a second term as prime minister in 1993.

Sadly, not everyone supported the democratic changes she had made. In December 2007, Bhutto was killed in a bomb attack while campaigning for a third term.

Bhutto's trip to the disputed Siachen glacier was symbolic of her life. She climbed to spectacular heights. She walked into dangerous territory in her quest for peace. And she listened patiently to the advice of others, knowing all the while that she had to rely on the secret strength she had within herself.

ICELAND IS CRUSHING THE GENDER GAP!

The tiny nation of Iceland has a population of around 330,000 people—and it is a great place to be a woman. In 1980 Vigdís Finnbogadóttir became the first woman in the world to be elected head of state. She served as president until 1996. From 2009 to 2012 Iceland had a female prime minister, Jóhanna Sigurðardóttir. And in 2016 Iceland elected a record number of women to Parliament: 30 of its 63 members. For the past nine years, Iceland's gender equality has been ranked number one in the world by the World Economic Forum.

Chapter 2

WOMEN WHO RULED IN POLITICS

What does it take to represent a nation? In democratic countries, it takes the confidence of the people. Each one of these women knew what it was to win the votes of her male and female citizens. And each entered a field dominated by male leaders who were not accustomed to women in positions of power. These women broke new ground, showing people what it's like when women run the world.

Ellen Johnson Sirleaf
(1938–)
President of Liberia

The African nation of Liberia is full of dramatic differences: Coastal cities and dense rain forests, indigenous African people and descendants of American slaves. Valuable natural resources and human poverty. Few leaders could unite a country as divided as Liberia has been. But as the first democratically

Ellen Johnson Sirleaf, 2013

elected female head of state in all of Africa, President Ellen Johnson Sirleaf has proven herself skilled at bringing Liberia's people together.

As a girl, Sirleaf watched both of her parents become leaders in a diverse community. Her father was a lawyer and member of the legislature. Her mother was, for a time, a traveling minister. Sirleaf's family dined with President Hilary Johnson, Liberia's first native-born president. But they also ate with villagers in remote parts of the country.

Sirleaf married and had children early. But unlike many women of her era, she also pursued her education. She traveled to the United States and studied to become an accountant and, later on, an economist. When she returned to Liberia, she worked in the Treasury Department. She

YEARS SERVED BY FEMALE HEADS OF STATE OR GOVERNMENT, 1964-2017

15+ Years	5
10-14	10
5-9	13
<1-4	42
0	77
No Data	

Most of the world's nations have never had a female leader.

bravely criticized policies that kept Liberia poor and underdeveloped.

In 1980 the president of Liberia, William Tolbert, was assassinated. The military staged a coup, taking over the government. Sirleaf was jailed and narrowly escaped death. She fled the country, but continued to work for the benefit of Liberia and other African nations in the United Nations Development Program.

Years of intense civil war followed. Then, in 2005, a free election took place, and Sirleaf became president. In her two terms, she drastically reduced Liberia's national debt. She worked to heal the war-torn nation. In 2011 Sirleaf was awarded the Nobel Peace Prize for her work in improving the lives of women.

Michelle Bachelet announcing her cabinet members before taking office as Chile's new president, January 2014

Michelle Bachelet
(1951–)
President of Chile

In the dark hours of September 11, 1973, soldiers under the command of Chilean dictator Augusto Pinochet raided the home of well-known Air Force General Alberto Bachelet. For the next several months, they questioned and tortured him, finally releasing him several months later. Weakened by the abuse, General Bachelet's heart gave out. Like thousands of other victims of Pinochet's rule, he died in custody. Not long afterward, Pinochet's soldiers arrested and interrogated General Bachelet's wife and daughter, and then forced them into exile.

The interrogators could not have known that Michelle Bachelet, the daughter of the slain general, would someday become Chile's first woman president.

Michelle Bachelet returned to Chile as a pediatrician. She specialized in treating the children of those who had disappeared under Pinochet. When Pinochet was ousted in 1973, Bachelet continued working to heal the country he had torn apart.

In 2000 President Ricardo Lagos appointed her Minister of Health. She worked to create a health system that guaranteed good health care for everyone, including the poor. In two years, she reduced the waiting list for doctors' appointments by 82 percent.

Because of Bachelet's success in changing the health system, Lagos appointed her Minister of Defense. She was the first woman in Latin America to hold such a position in the military. But her new role brought her face to face with people from her past. She was riding the same elevator as the man who had ordered her tortured when she was being held by Pinochet.

She made an important decision. She would not seek revenge. She later told reporters that Chileans might never agree about what had happened in their past, but they all had to work together to create a better future. As Minister of Defense, she reformed the way the military interacted with the public. Instead of being used to oppress people, the military rescued victims of floods and earthquakes.

In 2006 the people of Chile elected

Bachelet president. She served two terms: 2006 to 2010 and 2013 to 2017. During her presidency, she appointed the same number of female cabinet members as she appointed males. She helped enact laws that guaranteed equal wages for male and female employees. She expanded free education. And she worked to protect Chile's environment, building South America's first geothermal energy plant and creating a 286,000-square-mile (460,272-square-km) marine reserve around Easter Island.

Madeleine Albright

(1937–)
U.S. Secretary of State

Picture a train late at night, carrying two parents with two suitcases, hastily packed. With them is one small child. It is a story that played out thousands of times during the early years of World War II. In

Madeleine Albright was awarded the Presidential Medal of Freedom by President Barack Obama at the White House, May 2012.

this story, the little girl—Marie—would grow up in the United States. She would devote her life to preserving democracies all over the world.

Madeleine Albright, born Marie Jana Korbel, Czechoslovakia in 1937. When she was two years old, Nazi soldiers invaded her country. She and her parents fled. Almost every member of her family who stayed in Czechoslovakia died in concentration camps.

For many years, Albright's life followed the pattern customary for young women of her era: high school, college, then marriage and family. But Madeleine wanted more. In an early essay, she wrote "somehow it must be possible to be a responsible mother, a good wife, and have an intellectually satisfying job."

Albright found that satisfying job in international politics. She went to work first for Maine Senator Edmund Muskie while earning her PhD from Columbia University. After she earned her degree, Albright worked as an advisor to the National Security Council. In 1993 President Bill Clinton appointed her U.S. ambassador to the United Nations. She was almost always surrounded by male leaders when she worked there. She helped other leaders strengthen democracy in nations, including the Balkan countries of Eastern Europe.

In 1996 Albright was unanimously confirmed as U.S. Secretary of State, the highest-ranking woman in the nation's history. She helped strengthen democracy in countries that were once part of the communist Soviet Union, including Czechoslovakia. She participated in ground-breaking efforts to secure peace in the Middle East. She was the first secretary of state ever to meet with the leader of North Korea.

Madeleine Albright, a one-time refugee, dedicated her life to securing democracy worldwide. President Barack Obama awarded her the Presidential Medal of Freedom in 2012.

Shirley Chisholm
(1924–2005)
U.S. Representative

When Shirley Chisholm stepped to the podium in 1972 to announce that she was running for the U.S. presidency, she had already earned the support of thousands of Americans. Four years earlier, she had been elected to the U.S. House of Representatives. She was the first African American woman ever elected to Congress.

Standing behind the bristling microphones that day in 1972, Shirley Chisholm said, "I am not the candidate

Shirley Chisholm, 1970

of black America, though I am black and proud. I am not the candidate of the women's movement of this country, though I am a woman and equally proud of that. I am not the candidate of any political bosses or special interests. I am the people's candidate."

Chisholm learned to fight for the interests of the people in New York's neighborhoods, where she witnessed discrimination of all kinds. As a member of the New York State Assembly from 1964–1968, she rallied against unfair housing practices that left African Americans, Puerto Ricans, Jewish people, and poor people with few choices other than crowded tenements and public housing projects. She successfully sponsored laws that made unemployment benefits available to domestic workers. And she championed the SEEK program, which enabled disadvantaged students to succeed in college.

When she was elected to Congress in 1968, Chisholm was initially assigned to the House Agriculture Committee. In a shocking move for a newly elected representative, she demanded to be reassigned to a different committee—one where she could fight for the needs of her community. It worked. Challenging her assignment was just the first battle Chisholm fought. Sponsoring more than 50 pieces of legislation, she earned the nickname "fighting Shirley." She helped expand the food stamp program and start other programs that helped families feed their children. She made sure that the minimum wage applied to domestic workers. And she fought to end U.S. involvement in the Vietnam War.

Chisholm did not win the Democratic nomination in the 1972 presidential race. Most people believe that she never intended to win. She ran to awaken Americans to the possibility of an African American president, and a female one.

She once told reporters, "My greatest political asset, which professional politicians fear, is my mouth . . ." She left Congress after seven terms in office and began traveling the country teaching and giving lectures. For the rest of her life, she challenged people to change U.S. systems so that everyone would benefit from them.

Baroness Brenda Hale, DBE
(1945–)
President of the Supreme Court of England

Brenda Hale studied law at Cambridge University, where she experienced what it was like to be outnumbered. Of the 100 students

Brenda Hale, 2017

studying law, just six were female. Being one of just a few females may have been excellent training for her work in the British judiciary, where females make up just a tiny percentage of judges. After she graduated, she began teaching law at Manchester University. During her 18-year career as a professor, she wrote a book that explored how British law had treated women through the ages.

In 1984 Hale became the first woman appointed to the Law Commission, an organization that reforms outdated laws. She helped to modernize family law with the Children's Act of 1989. The new law made it clear how parents, the government, courts, and agencies would interact to protect children. She also helped change laws on divorce and mental health care.

In 2009 Lady Hale became the first woman ever appointed to the Supreme Court of the United Kingdom. Hale was named its president in 2017. That same year, a second female justice, Lady Black, was appointed to the Supreme Court. That meant that Lady Hale had female company on the court.

Lady Hale continues to press for greater diversity in the British judiciary. She told a group of female judges that a diverse court would enable people to "feel that the courts are their courts; that their cases are being decided and the law is being made by people like them."

The purpose of any human rights protection is to protect the rights of those whom the majority are unwilling to protect ...
—Brenda Hale

WOMEN ON THE U.S. SUPREME COURT

Justice Sandra Day O'Connor was the first woman appointed to the U.S. Supreme Court. She served from 1981 until she retired in 2006. She was awarded the Presidential Medal of Freedom, the nation's highest civilian honor, by President Barack Obama in 2009. Today, three women serve as associate justices on the U. S. Supreme Court. Justice Ruth Bader Ginsburg was appointed in 1993, Justice Sonia Sotomayor was appointed in 2009, and Justice Elena Kagan was appointed in 2010.

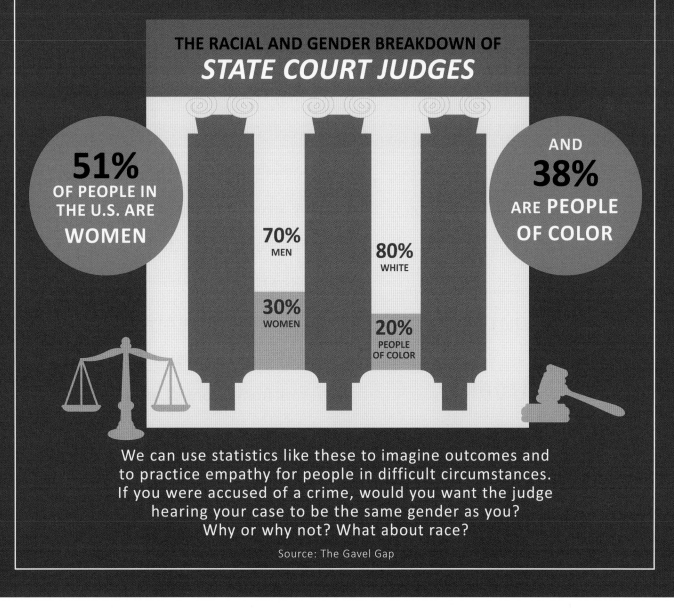

THE RACIAL AND GENDER BREAKDOWN OF
STATE COURT JUDGES

51% OF PEOPLE IN THE U.S. ARE **WOMEN**

70% MEN

30% WOMEN

80% WHITE

20% PEOPLE OF COLOR

AND **38%** ARE **PEOPLE OF COLOR**

We can use statistics like these to imagine outcomes and to practice empathy for people in difficult circumstances. If you were accused of a crime, would you want the judge hearing your case to be the same gender as you? Why or why not? What about race?

Source: The Gavel Gap

Chapter 3

WOMEN WHO RULED IN BUSINESS

Women who rule in business build financial empires. They create and save jobs. They bring new ideas, products, and services into the world. And they use their power, influence, and financial resources to lift up other people and make them successful too.

Elizabeth Arden
(1878–1966)
Founder of Elizabeth Arden, Inc.

In May 1912, 15,000 suffragettes marched in the streets of New York City.

They wore white dresses and sashes that read "Votes for Women." And many wore something else: red lipstick, supplied by an enterprising salon owner named Elizabeth Arden. The lipstick shade was "Red Door Red." It referred to the famous red door of Arden's Fifth Avenue salon.

Elizabeth Arden immigrated to New York from Toronto, Canada, where she had lived in poverty as a young girl. When her mother died of tuberculosis, Elizabeth set off for New York to earn a living. Without money or a college education, she took a

Elizabeth Arden, 1939

job at a beauty salon. That's where fortune turned its face toward her.

In 1910 Arden borrowed a small sum of money from her brother and opened her own beauty salon. She began creating her own line of beauty products. Inside the salon, clients received expensive facial treatments, massages, hair styling, and make-overs in a lavish spa environment. Before Elizabeth Arden entered the market, makeup was considered almost taboo. It was worn by stage actresses and movie stars. Arden made it acceptable—even glamorous—for everyone.

Elizabeth Arden had a special knack for marketing. During the Great Depression, when thousands of companies folded, Elizabeth Arden succeeded. The company had a profit of $4 million during the 1930s. During World War II she gave her lipsticks special names like "Victory Red," which made wearing them seem patriotic.

Elizabeth Arden was a fearsome boss. She paid her employees well but insisted that they work as hard as she did. She was also an innovator: first to offer travel sizes, first to send women door to door to demonstrate products, and first to incorporate the founder's name into the product line.

More than 100 years have passed since Elizabeth Arden distributed lipstick to New York City's suffragettes. Today, there are Red Door Spas worldwide, and the company generates revenues of $966 million a year.

Ursula Burns
(1958–)
First Female Chief Executive Officer (CEO) of a Fortune 500 Company

Ursula Burns grew up in the Baruch Houses—public housing on New York City's Delancey Street. At the time, the area was populated by African American, Jewish, and Hispanic families —almost all of them poor. Burns' mother operated a daycare business in her home. To bring in extra money, she ironed other people's clothes. Though she struggled at times to keep everyone fed, Burns' mother managed to send her three children to Catholic school. Ursula excelled in math.

"Many people told me I had three strikes against me," Burns said. "I was black. I was a girl. And I was poor."

The accepted path for Burns would have been to become a nurse or a teacher. But Burns longed to be an engineer. She graduated from the New York Polytechnic Institute in 1980 and from New York's Columbia University in 1981. Then she landed an internship at Xerox, a company well known for its copier machines. That internship led to a job.

One day early in her career, Burns did

Ursula Burns, 2014

something that showed Xerox executives what a strong leader she would become. In a large meeting, someone asked the vice president why Xerox was so focused on hiring women and people of color. Burns thought the vice president should not have dignified the question with an answer.

She stood up in the meeting and told the vice president that his answer showed a lack of passion and principles. Burns' decision to speak up paid off. She and the vice president kept talking. Their conversation led to a better position, and she was on her way.

"I learned from my mother that if you have a chance to speak, you should speak," she later said in an interview. Burns said she had learned growing up on Delancey Street that if you did not speak out, "you could really be run over."

In 2009 Ursula Burns became CEO of Xerox, making her the first African American to earn the top slot at a Fortune 500 company in the United States. In that position she handled tough negotiations with unions. She brought the company out of difficult financial times. And she helped engineer its transition from a copier business into a digital communications giant.

Today, Ursula Burns has retired from Xerox, but she continues to make an impact on corporate America. She is now on the board of directors of Uber, the ride-sharing company.

Sheryl Sandberg
(1969–)
Chief Operating Officer of Facebook

When she was growing up, Sheryl Sandberg's family valued hard work, education, and helping other people. This last value, helping others, grew from an idea central to their Jewish faith: *tikkun olam*, or "repairing the world." Sandberg has described how her grandmother sold watches out of the trunk of her car to raise money for the clinic that treated her breast cancer. And her parents carried on a long campaign to free persecuted Jews in the Soviet Union.

It is not surprising that helping others is pixelated throughout Sandberg's career. After earning a degree in economics from Harvard University in 1991, she took a job at World Bank. She wanted to help the bank achieve its mission of decreasing global poverty. Sandberg's job was researching data, but she did have a chance to see what the numbers meant in the real world. She traveled to clinics in remote parts of India, where World Bank funds helped people suffering from the disease of leprosy.

She went back to Harvard to get an advanced degree in business. Then, in 1996, she was hired as chief of staff for the U.S. Secretary of the Treasury. But political jobs like that one often change hands when a new president is elected. When a Republican president was elected in 2000, Sheryl decided to take a risk and join the private sector.

She accepted a job at what was then a budding tech company called Google in 2001. And for six years, during its

At a press conference in Paris in 2017, Sheryl Sandberg announced that Facebook would help support start-up tech companies.

meteoric rise, she was vice president of global online sales and operations.

It was her next job, however, that made her a household name. Facebook's founder, Mark Zuckerberg, met her at a Christmas party in 2008. Recognizing her intelligence and drive, Zuckerberg named her chief operating officer of Facebook. Today she runs the business side of the social media company, so developers can focus on what Facebook can do for the 2 billion people who use it every month.

Carrying on her family's tradition, Sandberg has used what she learned leading Google and Facebook to help other people, especially women. Her book *Lean In* sparked a nationwide movement to help millions of women overcome the barriers that stop them from achieving the success they would like to have in business.

Indra Nooyi
(1955–)
CEO of PepsiCo

In the last decade Indra Nooyi has been mentioned in nearly every published list of the world's most powerful women. She is the chief executive officer of Pepsico, the second largest food company in the world. She is responsible for more than 260,000 employees. And the company she runs generates $63.5 billion in revenues every year.

Indra Nooyi is a powerhouse.

As a child, she was held to high standards. Her grandfather waited at the door for her monthly report card, and woe be unto her if she did not achieve the highest grades. Her mother had high expectations as well. At dinner every night, Indra and her sister regularly gave speeches about how they would change India if they were named president or prime minister. Their mother would then announce which of them had won her vote.

After she graduated with degrees in physics, chemistry, and mathematics from Madras Christian College in India,

Nooyi made a daring decision. She would leave her home in tropical southern India and pursue an advanced degree at Yale University in the United States. It was a difficult path. She worked throughout graduate school, and once her bills were paid each month, she often had just a few dollars left over.

Today, Indra Nooyi speaks to business leaders worldwide. When she talks about what it took to become CEO of a major corporation, she is honest about the obstacles she faced. She makes it clear that because she was an immigrant and a woman, her work had to be twice as good as the work of men, and those born in the United States.

Indra Nooyi, 2016

"One of the things my parents and my grandfather taught me was when you do a job you have got to do it better than everybody else," she told an interviewer. "Simple. I just don't know any other way to work."

Susan Wojcicki, 2017

Susan Wojcicki
(1968–)
CEO of YouTube

Two guys in orange Rockets jerseys are lip-synching a Backstreet Boys song. They fake-wail, execute choreographed moves, and in the background, their roommate never stops doing his homework. This video is the one that convinced Susan Wojcicki that the online platform YouTube was going to be big. Millions of people all over the world were watching the lip-synching duo.

Watching YouTube's growth skyrocket was not Wojcicki's first experience with a tech startup. Google's founders started their business in her garage in Menlo Park, California. She remembers the late night pizza-and-M&M-fueled talks that led to the company's creation. Not only was Wojcicki their first landlord, she was Google's 16th employee.

At Google, she developed the advertising sales programs that generate billions for the company. And she championed the deal when Google bought YouTube in 2006. Fast forward eight years—and Susan became CEO at YouTube. Her aim was to increase revenue from ad sales as much as she had at Google. So far, her love of YouTube celebrities and her desire to see them succeed are doing the trick. YouTube is now worth $90 billion.

Susan is a master at making profits, but she also uses her influence to change the lives of those around her. At Google, she set up the company's famous in-house daycare for the children of employees. She advocated for paid maternity leave. And she uses her platform to challenge employers to hire more women in every field.

This dedication to social good may have its roots in her upbringing. She grew up on the campus of Stanford University, where her dad was a physics professor. She was surrounded by passionate scholars. She says, "Their goal wasn't to become famous or make money, it was to do something that was meaningful for the world because they had a passion."

DO WOMEN'S COLLEGES PREPARE WOMEN TO LEAD?

Most students in the U.S. and UK choose to attend coeducational schools. But are there advantages to being educated in a women-only environment? Studies show that women-only colleges educate only about 2 percent of students, but 33 percent of the women board members of Fortune 500 companies were educated in women-only colleges. Students who attend women-only colleges are also twice as likely to earn a PhD.

This image, published in Business Insider Magazine, *shows the percentage of women in leadership roles in businesses worldwide. Which figure surprises you the most?*
Source: Business Insider

Chapter 4

WOMEN WHO RULED IN COMMUNICATION

In many ways, the women who rule in media are world-builders. They shape the way we see the world through news reporting. They create fictional worlds through art, music, and fashion. Each one of these women inspires people to speak, to write, and to live in a way that changes the world we share.

Katharine Graham
(1917–2001)
Publisher, *Washington Post*

Katharine Graham once said that success often came down to luck. In many ways, she was a lucky woman. Katharine was born into a wealthy family—one that operated the thriving *Washington Post* newspaper. Yet, in some

Katharine Graham, 1980

ways, she was unlucky. Men in her family viewed women as having limited abilities. When her father was ready to retire, instead of trusting the paper to Katharine, he passed it to her husband, Philip, who struggled with mental illness and was unkind to Katharine.

In 1963 Philip took his own life. Katharine felt she had three choices: sell the paper, find someone else to operate it, or run the *Washington Post* herself. Trembling, shy, and terrified of public speaking, she decided to captain the paper. She was the first woman to take control of a major newspaper in the United States.

It was the first of many tough decisions she faced. In 1971 Daniel Ellsberg leaked documents that showed the government had lied about American involvement in the Vietnam War. Graham decided to publish those papers, even though the government threatened to charge her with a crime. She took the risk because she believed in the importance of a free press. Later, she and her editors decided to investigate a plot to break into Democratic Party headquarters in the Watergate Hotel. The reporting of the *Washington Post* led to the resignation of President Nixon, who was threatened with impeachment for obstruction of justice.

For its daring investigative reporting under Graham's leadership, the *Washington Post* received the Pulitzer Prize. The newspaper also became one of the most respected news sources in the world. In 1971 the paper's stock sold for $26 per share. In 1991, after 20 years of Katharine's guidance, shares sold for $222 each, an increase of more than 750 percent.

Oprah Winfrey

(1954–)
Media mogul and philanthropist

When Oprah Winfrey was a child, she was dismayed by the food that came from her grandmother's garden. Eating homegrown crowder peas and collards made her feel poor. She wanted something different. Oprah was already showing a tendency that would shape her whole life: a refusal to live within the limitations others placed on her.

Oprah left rural Mississippi when she was six years old. She went to live with her mother, but she suffered extreme abuse there. She moved to Nashville, Tennessee, to live with her dad. In her teenage years, her refusal to accept limitations led to trouble, but eventually she found her way to college and into a career in broadcasting.

In 1984 she began hosting a television talk show called *AM Chicago*. She was the

Oprah Winfrey attended the 2015 Film Independent Spirit Awards held at Santa Monica Beach in California.

first African American woman to host her own talk show. Shortly afterward, it became *The Oprah Winfrey Show*. When her show was syndicated nationally in 1986, Winfrey asked her boss to give the members of her team a raise. He said there was no need because they were "all girls." Once again, Winfrey bristled at the unfair limitation. In 1986 she formed Harpo Productions and took control of her own show. Ratings soared. Winfrey ended her show—having been the highest-rated talk show of all time—in 2011.

Winfrey has since ventured into other fields. She acts. She produces movies and Broadway musicals. In 2011, she started the Oprah Winfrey Network. During her career, she has won Emmy awards for her work in television, Academy Awards for her work in movies, and a Tony award for her work in theater. In 2013 President Obama awarded her the Presidential Medal of Freedom.

Today, Oprah Winfrey is regarded as one of the most influential people in the world. Her net worth is more than $2.8 billion. She has donated millions to charities worldwide, including the boarding school she established for underprivileged girls in South Africa.

J.K. Rowling
(1965–)
Author, *Harry Potter* series

Joanne Rowling grew up in England and Wales, surrounded by books. She was, she says, a classic "bookworm, complete with freckles and National Health Service spectacles." She began writing her own novels when she was still a child.

She penned the *Harry Potter* books when she lived in Scotland. While she worked as a teacher, she plotted and drafted the series over the course of five years, in spare moments and on scribbled scraps of paper. The manuscript of the first book, *Harry Potter and the Sorcerer's Stone*, was rejected many times, but her story finally found a home at Bloomsbury Books. When it was published in 1997, it shattered sales records in the UK, the U.S., and across the globe. Kids and adults lined up to purchase each new volume in the series as it came out. The books led to movies and merchandise. Eventually, they gave birth to a thriving online community of Muggle-born fans.

Harry Potter is a fantasy series, but its effects on publishing and tourism are real. Reports estimate that its popularity has led to a ten-fold increase in the number of children's books published every year. Today, children's books outsell adult books in the United States. Potter fans flock to London and to theme parks in the United States to experience real-life recreations of Hogwarts, Diagon Alley, and Platform

J.K. Rowling, 2017

9 3/4 at Kings Cross Station in London.

In *Harry Potter and the Sorcerer's Stone*, as Harry steels himself to pass through black flames and face his enemy, he

Anna Wintour, 2017

admits to his friend Hermione that she is the better wizard. Hermione brushes off his praise.

"Me!" said Hermione. "Books! And cleverness! There are more important things . . ."

Like the witch she famously created, J.K. Rowling may credit her powers to books and cleverness. But the worlds she created in the *Harry Potter* books are magic to millions of child and adult readers all over the world.

Anna Wintour
(1949–)
Artistic Director, Condé Nast Publications

In each of the world's fashion capitals—Paris, London, New York, Milan—one week of the year supersedes all others. During Fashion Week, designers, models, stylists, photographers, and celebrities gather to present the new clothing collections, and everyone hungers for the approval of one woman.

She arrives at the runway shows early. Her signature pageboy hair barely brushes the frames of her sunglasses. She is Dame Anna Wintour. For 30 years, she has run the world's most famous fashion magazine: *Vogue*. In its 125-year history, the magazine has never had a more influential editor than Wintour.

She is famously hands-on. As editor-in-chief, she approves color palettes, trends, faces—every detail presented to the public. She is as fierce a guardian of the magazine's words as she is of its images. With Wintour at the helm, *Vogue's* influence on what people wear—and on what people think is beautiful—is enormous.

Wintour grew up in London in the 1960s. She stepped into the fashion world at a pivotal moment in history. Women were entering the working world in larger numbers, earning their own money, and enjoying new personal freedoms. She put fashion and faces that celebrated this new independence on the pages of *Vogue*.

"Seeing that revolution go on made me love fashion from an early age," she said.

In 2013 Wintour expanded her influence on publishing. She was named artistic director of Condé Nast, the publishing company that owns *Vogue*. Condé Nast also owns *Vanity Fair, Glamour, The New Yorker, Architectural Digest, Bon Appétit,* and *Wired*—magazines that reach more than 120 million consumers worldwide. In 2014 Queen Elizabeth II conferred the title Dame on Wintour in recognition of her contribution to the world of fashion.

Beyoncé Knowles, 2013

Beyoncé Knowles
(1981–)
Writer, Singer, Producer, Actor

From the walls of her childhood home in Houston, Texas, a sisterhood of beautiful black women surrounded Beyoncé Knowles. The paintings in her mother's collection showed her what daring art looked like. It was a lesson she learned well.

Knowles began performing at the age of seven. When she was 16, she signed with Columbia Records as part of the three-member group, *Destiny's Child*. Their albums sold more than 60 million copies. By 2003 she had embarked on a solo career. Both commercial and critical success followed. *Rolling Stone* magazine said her vocals were "shifting the entire landscape of R&B."

But money and fame were not enough. She wanted independence. For that, she had to make a painful decision: to step out on her own, without her father as manager. Their separation caused a rift between them, but it liberated Knowles to set new goals. Her albums *4, Beyoncé,* and *Lemonade* followed, each one achieving greater acclaim than the one before. *Lemonade,* in particular, was praised for its fierce feminism and frank critique of racism. The Formation tour that followed was criticized by some who took offense at its positive references to the Black Panthers, but many people found it empowering.

Knowles' albums have debuted six times at number one on the Billboard charts—something no other artist has done. She has performed at the Super Bowl twice, and she sang the national anthem at the inauguration of President Obama. Her work has given rise to a $350 million empire: films, celebrity endorsements, clothing and fragrance lines, plus countless philanthropic acts.

When Knowles announced in 2016 that she was carrying twins, Warsan Shire wrote a poem for her titled "I Have Three Hearts." For anyone looking at the scope, the depth, and the passion of Knowles' work, that seems about right.

> *Do what you were born to do. You just have to trust yourself.*
> —Beyoncé Knowles

Chapter 5

WOMEN WHO RULED IN SPORTS

These women are game changers. Each one was blessed with superior athletic talent. Each one broke records in her sport. But they did something else as well: In different ways, they opened the realm of sports to generations of young women who might otherwise have been left out.

Abby Wambach
(1980–)
Highest-scoring soccer player in the world

Few female soccer players have amassed the titles Abby Wambach has won. World Cup Champion. Two-time Olympic gold medalist. FIFA World Soccer Player of the Year in 2012. Six-time U.S. Soccer Athlete of the Year. Highest all-time scorer on the U.S. Women's National Team. And then there is the fact that no one, male or female, has ever scored more international goals than she has: 184 in her career.

But titles, trophies, and statistics are only part of what makes this woman a champion. Her ferocity on the field has inspired a generation of young female

Abby Wambach during the China versus U.S. women's soccer match in 2015

soccer players. Once, during a crucial match against Mexico in the World Cup, she leapt up to head the ball and connected instead with another player. With blood pouring from her injured forehead, she ran to the sidelines, had medics staple the wound closed, and then raced back into the game. Her intensity helped redefine what it means to play like a girl.

And she's had nearly as many victories off the field as she's had on. Wambach used her famously loud voice to fight for gender equality in the sport of soccer. She and her teammates led the drive for women's soccer teams to be treated the same as men's teams by FIFA, the international governing body of the sport of soccer. When FIFA announced that important women's games would be played on Astroturf instead of real grass, Wambach and her teammates filed a lawsuit to prevent the unfair and dangerous change in turf.

They fought to practice on the same quality equipment and in the same quality facilities as the men's teams use. They campaigned to raise women players' salaries. Even though women's soccer teams won more championships, men's teams still earned more money when they lost than women's teams earned when they won. Wambach and her teammates proved that fierce advocacy works. In 2017 the U.S. Women's soccer team negotiated a contract that dramatically increased their pay and improved their working conditions.

Scoring 184 career goals is a stunning accomplishment. But her campaign to empower girls and women in the sport may outlast her scoring record. She taught a nation of girls and young women to pursue their goals with relentless ferocity, both on and off the field.

Misty Copeland
(1980–)
Principal dancer, American Ballet Theater

Some people are born into wealth and that makes rising to greatness easier. That was not the case for Misty Copeland. When she was a child, her mother worked hard but struggled to earn enough to take care of Misty and her five siblings. Sometimes there were no beds to sleep in. Sometimes they bought food with coins they found under the sofa cushions. But Misty had gifts of another kind. She had an uncommon talent for dancing.

Her natural ability was spotted by a volunteer dance teacher at the Boys & Girls Club in her neighborhood. Misty started dancing when she was 13, years later than most professional dancers. But she picked up movements quickly. She was as flexible as a pipe cleaner. And

Misty Copeland, 2015

she spent hours practicing. *Plié. Tendu. Battement.* Every sweep of her slipper built strength, precision, and grace.

The instructor at the Boys & Girls Club offered Copeland classes in a private studio. She invited Copeland to live in her home so she could focus on dance. From there, Copeland's determination and talent opened one door after another, from San Francisco Ballet to the American Ballet Theater's summer intensive program. Then she studied at the American Ballet Theater's studio company. And after that, a position in the American Ballet Theater's corps de ballet. She danced every coveted role in classical ballet—Clara in *The Nutcracker*, Odette in *Swan Lake*, Juliet in *Romeo & Juliet*—and many times she was the first African American woman to do so. There were times when people told her she had grown too curvy to dance those classical roles. There were times she was desperately lonely as the only African American female in the company. There were times she was sidelined by injury. But she persevered. *Plié. Tendu. Battement.*

In 2015 Misty Copeland was promoted to principal dancer in the American Ballet Theater. She is the first black woman ever to rise to that position in the company. Her presence on stage, dancing these coveted roles, shows African American girls that ballet is for everyone.

Pat Summitt
(1952–2016)
Coach of University of Tennessee's Lady Vols

Some of the most influential people in sports are the coaches that bring out the greatness in others. Pat Summitt is one of those people in the history of basketball.

She has been described as a hurricane: a force of nature that drove teams to victory. In her 38-year coaching career, Summitt never had a losing season. She won 1,098 games, more than any other NCAA Division I basketball coach, male or female. She led her teams to eight NCAA national championships, the most for any women's basketball coach in history. She won National Coach of the Year seven times.

And Pat was a fierce athlete herself. She won an Olympic silver medal in 1976, the first time women's basketball was played as an Olympic sport. Eight years later, she coached the U.S. team that won the gold.

Though she was renowned for her steely glare and fierce tactics, Summitt was loved with equal ferocity. In 2011, she was diagnosed with dementia, a disease that affects people's ability to remember. Near the end of her life, former players came from across the country to sit by her bedside. One of them, Sheila Collins, brought a letter Summitt had written to her before her first game. It read:

> *Winning is fun … Sure.*
>
> *But winning is not the point.*

Pat Summitt, 2012

> *Wanting to win is the point.*
>
> *Not giving up is the point.*
>
> *Never letting up is the point.*
>
> *Never being satisfied with what you've done is the point.*
>
> *The game is never over. No matter what the scoreboard reads, or what the referee says, it doesn't end when you come off the court.*

In 2012 President Obama awarded Summitt the nation's highest civilian honor: the Presidential Medal of Freedom.

Summitt's contribution to women's sports did not end when she left the court. It is a mark of her profound influence on basketball that more than 75 of her former players have gone on to become coaches themselves, passing the ball to future generations.

Wilma Rudolph
(1940–1994)
Olympic sprinter and civil rights activist

Wilma Rudolph was outrunning adversity from day one. She was born early, weighing little more than 4 pounds (1.8 kg). The nearest hospital refused to take care of Wilma and her mother because they were black. As a result, Wilma Rudolph fell ill and contracted polio.

Her doctor said she would never walk. But Wilma's mother insisted that she would, and Wilma believed her mama. She took off her leg brace by herself. She let her family members massage the leg that had been twisted by polio. By the age of 6 she was hopping around the house. By 11 she was playing basketball barefoot.

Well-known track coach Ed Temple noticed Rudolph's talent and began to train her. She ran in college track and field events though she was only in high school.

When Rudolph was 16 she competed in the 1956 Olympics in Melbourne, Australia. She won a bronze medal in the 400-meter relay. In 1960 she competed in the Rome Olympics. This time, she came home with three medals—all of them gold. She also broke three world records. Rudolph was being called "the fastest woman in the world."

When she returned to Tennessee, she faced the same racism that had resulted in

Wilma Rudolph is shown holding up the three gold medals she won at the 1960 Olympics in Rome.

her contracting polio earlier in her life. The parade planned in her honor would be segregated—no African Americans would be allowed to come. Rudolph got angry.

She refused to attend—and her protest worked. Her welcome home parade was the first integrated event in her town's history.

In 1983 Rudolph was inducted into the Olympic Hall of Fame. Historian Bud Greenspan said she had changed the world of sports forever.

Serena Williams
(1981–)
Champion tennis player

Serena Williams and her sister Venus grew up in Compton, a poor California neighborhood troubled by violence and drug use. But the Williams family had big aspirations for Venus and Serena. Venus says that at eight years old, she announced the intention to win Wimbledon five times (she achieved that goal in 2008). Serena played extra hard because she felt she was a "runt." The hand skills she learned helped her compensate for her smaller size.

Serena Williams has won 23 Grand Slam titles in 29 singles matches, more than any other player—male or female—in the open era. She has won four Olympic gold medals, including three she shares with her sister Venus for doubles matches. Serena has earned nearly $85 million in prize money and has more than a dozen endorsement partners.

Her generosity is equally admirable. Serena has started schools in Kenya and Jamaica. She works with schools in Compton to keep them stocked with supplies. She established the Yetunde Price Resource Center, named for her elder sister, Yetunde, who died as a result of gun violence. The center offers help to those recovering from the effects of violence in the community.

Williams is a bold advocate for women of color everywhere. She said, "The cycles of poverty, discrimination, and sexism are much, much harder to break than the record for Grand Slam titles."

Serena Williams, 2016

Serena Williams has frequently held the top spot in her sport over the years. She has won more matches than anyone else in professional tennis. Her physical strength, the pinpoint accuracy of her serves, and the ferocious speed at which she propels a ball mean that she rules the court. And she rose to that position over obstacles that would have crushed a weaker person: race, money, gender. None of them was a match for her. And for those reasons, many people say Serena Williams is the best athlete of all time.

Timeline

1910 Elizabeth Arden opens her beauty salon

1912 15,000 suffragettes march in the streets of New York City

1953 Elizabeth II becomes queen of England

1963 Katharine Graham becomes President of the *Washington Post*

1968 Shirley Chisholm is elected to United States Congress

1972 Shirley Chisholm announces she is running for the United States Presidency

1976 Pat Summitt wins an Olympic silver medal in basketball

1979 Margaret Thatcher takes office as Prime Minister of Britain

1980 Ursula Burns graduates from the New York Polytechnic Institute

1981 Ursula Burns graduates from Columbia University

1981 Sandra Day O'Connor becomes the first woman appointed to the U.S. Supreme Court

1983 Shirley Chisholm finishes her terms as a U.S. Congresswoman

1984 Brenda Hale becomes first woman appointed to the Law Commission of England

1986 *The Oprah Winfrey Show* debuts

1988 Benazir Bhutto begins first term as Prime Minister of Pakistan

1990 Margaret Thatcher resigns as Prime Minister of Britain

1993 Benazir Bhutto begins second term as Prime Minister of Pakistan

1996 Madeleine Albright is confirmed as United States Secretary of State

1997 J.K. Rowling publishes her first *Harry Potter* book

2000 Michelle Bachelet becomes Minister of Health in Chile

2001 Sheryl Sandberg joins Google

2002 Michelle Bachelet becomes Minister of National Defense in Chile

2005 Angela Merkel is elected chancellor of Germany

2005 Ellen Johnson Sirleaf becomes president of Liberia

2006 Michelle Bachelet begins first term as President of Chile

2006 Indra Nooyi becomes President and CEO of PepsiCo

2008 Sheryl Sandberg named chief operating officer of Facebook

2009 Brenda Hale becomes first woman ever appointed to Supreme Court of the United Kingdom

2009 Ursula Burns becomes CEO of Xerox

2010 Michelle Bachelet ends first term as President of Chile

2011 Ellen Johnson Sirleaf awarded Nobel Peace Prize

2012 Madeleine Albright is awarded the Presidential Medal of Freedom

2012 Abby Wambach is named FIFA World Soccer Player of the Year

2012 Pat Summitt is awarded the Presidential Medal of Freedom

2013 Michelle Bachelet begins second term as President of Chile

2013 Anna Wintour becomes artistic director of Condé Nast

2014 Susan Wojcicki becomes CEO of YouTube

2015 Misty Copeland is promoted to principal dancer in the American Ballet Theater

2016 Beyoncé's album *Lemonade* is released

2016 Serena Williams wins her seventh Wimbeldon title

2017 Michelle Bachelet ends second term as President of Chile

2017 The U.S. Women's soccer team negotiates a contract that increases their pay and improves working conditions

Glossary

assassinate—to murder a leader for political or religious reasons

ceremony— special actions, words, or music performed to mark an important event

concentration camp— a camp where people such as prisoners of war, political prisoners, or refugees are held

corps de ballet—the group of primary performers in a ballet company

coup—a violent change in the leadership of a government, often by the military

democratic—a government in which the citizens elect the leaders

gender—the cultural or social behaviors associated with masculinity or femininity

House of Lords—the upper house of the British parliament

indigenous—native to a place

Parliament—a legislative body in government

persecute—to punish or treat badly for one's beliefs

recession—temporary slowing of business activity

refugee—a person who flees his or her homeland because of oppression or disaster

syndicate—a group of people involved in official business

Critical Thinking Questions

1. The author of this book used autobiographies and interviews with the women featured. What are some of the advantages of using these sources? What are the disadvantages of relying on the stories a person tells about her own life?
2. Compare the backgrounds of the women in this book. With such different life stories, what characteristics do these women share?
3. Modern culture supports male leaders being ambitious, assertive, and confident. When women display the same characteristics, they are seen differently. Why do you think this is the case? What might change that? How could changing our language habits encourage more girls to become leaders?

Further Reading

Caldwell, Stella A. *100 Women Who Made History: Remarkable Women Who Shaped Our World.* New York: DK Children. 2017.

Carmon, Iris and Iris Knizhzik. *Notorious RBG: The Life and Times of Ruth Bader Ginsburg,* New York: Harper Collins, 2017.

Ignotofsky, Rachel. *Women in Sports: 50 Fearless Athletes Who Played to Win.* New York: Ten Speed Press, 2017.

Schatz, Kate. *Rad American Women A-Z,* San Francisco: City Lights Books, 2015.

Internet Sites

Use Facthound to find Internet sites related to this book.

Visit *www.facthound.com*

Just type in 9780756558512 and go.

Source Notes

Page 8, col. 1, line 6: Chris Leadbeater. "The Queen's 90 Years – and 271 Foreign Trips." *Telegraph*. June 13, 2016, http://www.telegraph.co.uk/travel/news/Around-the-world-with-the-Queen/

Page 9, col. 2, line 1: Karl Vick. "TIME Person of the Year 2015: Angela Merkel." *TIME*. http://time.com/time-person-of-the-year-2015-angela-merkel/

Page 9, col. 1, line 11: "The Reunification of Germany." Encyclopedia Britannica. May 2, 2018, https://www.britannica.com/place/Germany/The-reunification-of-Germany

Page 10, col. 2, line 19: "Durga." Encyclopedia Britannica. July 21, 2017, https://www.britannica.com/topic/Durga

Page 15, col. 1, line 22: Jason Burke. "Benazir Bhutto." *The Guardian*. December 27, 2007, https://www.theguardian.com/world/2007/dec/28/pakistan.obituaries

Page 15, col. 1, line 8: Jane Perlez and Victoria Burnett. "Benazir Bhutto, 54, Lived in Eye of Pakistan Storm." *The New York Times*. December 28, 2007, http://www.nytimes.com/2007/12/28/world/asia/28bhuttocnd.html

Page 19, col. 1, line 17: Afua Hirsch. "Can Ellen Johnson Sirleaf Save Liberia?" *The Guardian*. 22 July 2017. https://www.theguardian.com/global-development/2017/jul/23/can-president-ellen-johnson-sirleaf-save-liberia

Page 19, col. 1, line 20: "Ellen Johnson Sirleaf — Facts." Nobel Prize Organization. https://www.nobelprize.org/nobel_prizes/peace/laureates/2011/johnson_sirleaf-facts.html

Page 20, col. 1, line 9: Larry Rohter. "Chile Inagurates First Woman to Serve as Its President." *The New York Times*. March 12, 2006, http://www.nytimes.com/2006/03/12/world/americas/chile-inaugurates-first-woman-to-serve-as-its-president.html

Page 20, col. 2, line 12: "Chilean President Speaks of her Torture Under Pinochet." Yahoo. November 14, 2014, https://www.yahoo.com/news/chilean-president-speaks-her-torture-under-pinochet-192814454.html

Page 23, col.1, line 21: "Shirley Chisholm Biography." Biography. https://www.biography.com/people/shirley-chisholm-9247015

Page 24, col. 1, line 10: "Shirley Chisholm, Pioneer in Congress, Dies at 80." NBC News. January 4, 2005, http://www.nbcnews.com/id/6779424/#.VUUPjPlViko

Page 26, col. 1, line 20: "Baroness Hale Appointed as UK's First Female Top Judge." *BBC*. July 21, 2017, http://www.bbc.com/news/uk-40679293

Page 26, col. 1, line 11: Clare Dyer. "The Guardian Profile: Lady Brenda Hale." *The Guardian*. January 9, 2004,

https://www.theguardian.com/uk/2004/jan/09/lords.women

Page 30, col. 2, line 11: Faith Dallal. "100 Years Behind the Iconic Red Door." *Vanity Fair*. November 8, 2010, https://www.vanityfair.com/style/2010/11/100-years-behind-the-iconic-red-door

Page 31, col. 2, line 3: Kathleen Elkins. "How Calling Out a VP Helped an Entry-Level Employee Become CEO of Xerox." CNBC. February 7, 2017, https://www.cnbc.com/2017/02/07/calling-out-a-vp-helped-an-entry-level-employee-become-ceo-of-xerox.html

Page 32, col. 1, line 13: "Ursula Burns: CEO, Xerox Corporation." Makers. https://www.makers.com/profiles/591f28b1bea177748042171a

Page 34, col. 2, line 20: "Indra Nooyi." Encyclopedia Britannica. November 22, 2017, https://www.britannica.com/biography/Indra-Nooyi

Page 51, col. 1, line 21: "Discover Misty's Journey." The Official Website of Misty Copeland. http://mistycopeland.com/about/

Page 53, col. 1, line 7: Sally Jenkins. "'The Game is Never Over': A Letter from Pat Summitt to a Young Basketball Player." *The Washington Post*. June 28, 2016, https://www.washingtonpost.com/sports/colleges/widely-beloved-pat-summitt-was-cherished-most-by-those-who-saw-her-complexities/2016/06/28/581a391a-3d2e-11e6-80bc-d06711fd2125_story.html?tid=a_inl&utm_term=.9fbe7df82476

page 54, col. 1, line 1: Gary Smith. "Eyes of the Storm." *Sports Illustrated*. Mar 2, 1998, https://www.si.com/vault/1998/03/02/239460/eyes-of-the-storm-when-tennessees-whirlwind-of-a-coach-pat-summitt-hits-you-with-her-steely-gaze-you-get-a-dose-of-the-intensity-that-has-carried-the-lady-vols-to-five-ncaa-titles

Page 54, col. 2, line 12: KeriLynn Engel. "Wilma Rudolph, Olympic Gold Medalist & Civil Rights Pioneer." Amazing Women in History. August 14, 2012, http://www.amazingwomeninhistory.com/wilma-rudolph-olympic-gold-medalist-civil-right-pioneer/

Page 54, col. 2, line 21: Frank Litsky. "Wilma Rudolph, Star of the 1960 Olympics, Dies at 54." *The New York Times*. 1994. http://www.nytimes.com/1994/11/13/obituaries/wilma-rudolph-star-of-the-1960-olympics-dies-at-54.html

Page 55, col. 2, line 2: Barbara Heilman. "Like Nothing Else in Tennessee." *Sports Illustrated*. November 14, 1960, https://www.si.com/vault/1960/11/14/585203/like-nothing-else-in-tennessee

All Internet sites were accessed on May 11, 2018.

Select Bibliography

Bedell Smith, Sally. *Elizabeth the Queen*. New York: Random House, 2012.

Bhutto, Benazir. *Daughter of Destiny*. New York: Harper Collins, 2008.

Chisholm, Shirley. *Unbought & Unbossed*. Ontario, Canada: Take Root Media Edition. 2010.

Copeland, Misty and Charisse Jones. *Life in Motion*. New York: Scholastic, Inc., 2014

Johnson Sirleaf, Ellen. *This Child Will Be Great*. New York: Harper Perennial, 2009.

Malhotra, Inder. *Indira Gandhi, A Personal and Political Biography*. Boston, Mass.: Northeastern University Press, 2012.

Muñoz, Heraldo. *Getting Away With Murder: Benazir Bhutto's Assassination and the Politics of Pakistan*. New York: W. W. Norton & Company, 2013.

Qvortrup, Matthew. *Angela Merkel: Europe's Most Influential Leader*. New York: Overlook Duckworth, 2016.

Thatcher, Margaret. *The Autobiography*. New York: Harper Perennial, 2013.

Wambach, Abby. *Forward*. New York: Harper Collins, 2016.

Winfrey, Oprah. *What I Know for Sure*. New York: Flatiron Books, 2014

Woodhead, Lindy. *War Paint*. Hoboken, N.J.: Wiley, 2008

About the Author

Rebecca Stanborough obtained her BA from Agnes Scott College, a women's college in Decatur, Georgia. She also earned an MFA in Writing for Children and Adults from Minnesota's Hamline University. Rebecca is the author of four other books for young readers, and her short story "The Latter Days of Jean" appeared in the Capstone anthology *Love & Profanity*. She writes and teaches in St. Augustine, Florida.

Index